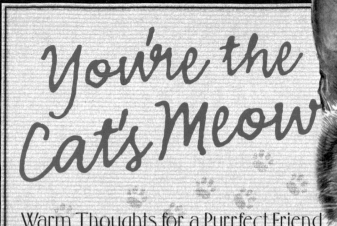

You're the Cat's Meow

Warm Thoughts for a Purrfect Friend

Artwork by Debbie Cook

HARVEST HOUSE PUBLISHERS

EUGENE, OREGON

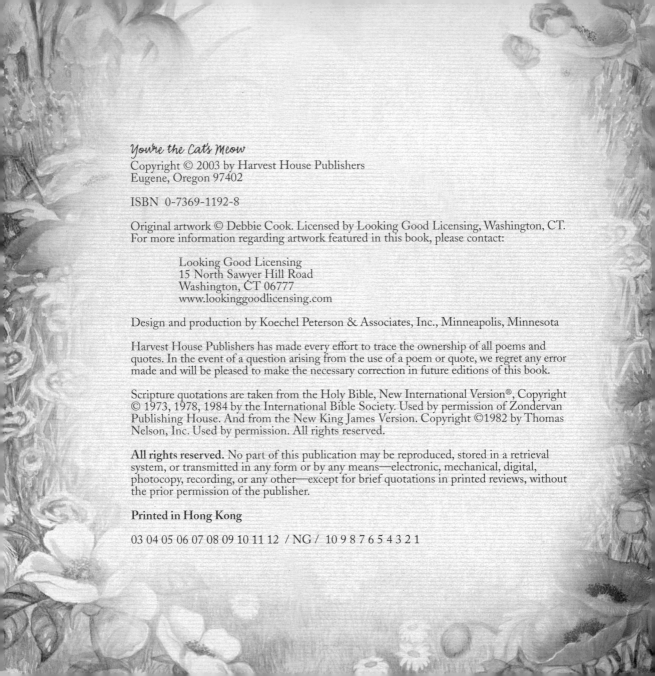

If we treated everyone we meet with the same affection
we bestow upon our favorite cat, they, too, would purr.

LEWIS CARROLL

Love is all very well in its way,
but friendship is much higher.
Indeed, I know of nothing in the world that is
either nobler or rarer than a devoted friendship.

OSCAR WILDE

You just remind me of what's really important in life,
friends, best friends.

FANNIE FLAGG
The Whistle Stop Café

To gain the friendship of a cat is a difficult thing. The cat is a philosophical, methodical, quiet animal, tenacious of its own habits, fond of order and cleanliness, and it does not lightly confer its friendship. If you are worthy of its affection, a cat will be your friend, but never your slave. He keeps his free will, though he loves, and he will not do for you what he thinks is unreasonable. But if he once gives himself to you, it is with absolute confidence and affection.

THEOPHILE GAUTIER

Dear friend, I pray that you may enjoy good health
and that all may go well with you,
even as your soul is getting along well.

THE BOOK OF 3 JOHN

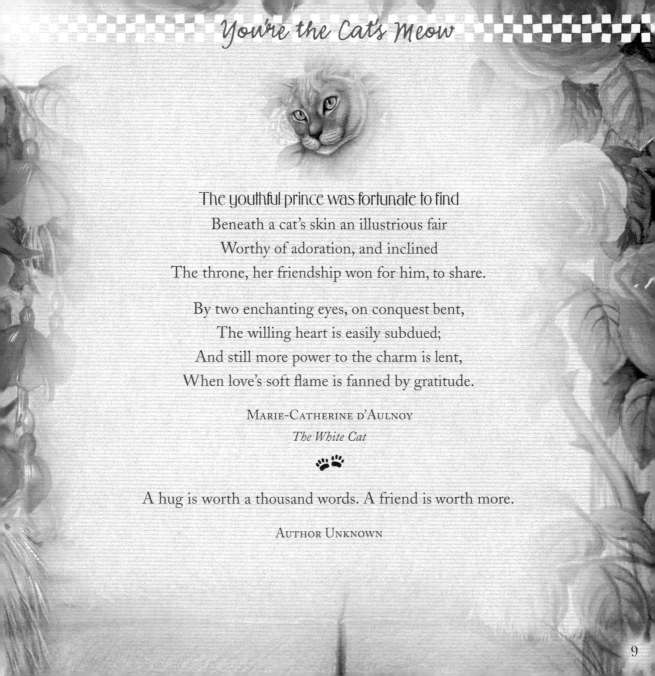

The youthful prince was fortunate to find
Beneath a cat's skin an illustrious fair
Worthy of adoration, and inclined
The throne, her friendship won for him, to share.

By two enchanting eyes, on conquest bent,
The willing heart is easily subdued;
And still more power to the charm is lent,
When love's soft flame is fanned by gratitude.

MARIE-CATHERINE D'AULNOY
The White Cat

A hug is worth a thousand words. A friend is worth more.

AUTHOR UNKNOWN

So Earnest threw some more wood upon the fire; and then, seating himself upon a great block in the opposite chimney corner, leaned his elbows upon his knees and took an attentive survey of his visitor, who, having completed her preening, sat regarding the fire with half-closed eyes, purring softly a little tune of her own composition, and beating time with her long tail.

She was a very pretty cat, with fur of rich dark gray, except her paws and face, which were pure white, and a crown or circle about her head, of an indescribable glittering appearance. It was this crown-like circle which had induced Earnest to call her highness and queen.

JANE AUSTEN
The Gray Cat

Friendship only is, indeed, genuine when two friends,
without speaking a word to each other,
can nevertheless find happiness in being together.

GEORGE EBER

As the feast continued the cats curled up contentedly on their cushions and suddenly from all three came a pleasant hum. It was the wonderful, happy sound of purring, the reward, the cats explained to the princess, they had received for their help to her. Strangely enough the sound was very much like the whir and hum of a spinning wheel. And from that day to this cats have continued to purr whenever they feel contented.

AUTHOR UNKNOWN
Three White Cats

Yesterday brought the beginning,
tomorrow brings the end, but somewhere in the middle
we've become best of friends.

AUTHOR UNKNOWN

For all their fabled aloofness, our cats turn out to be quite warm and friendly.
Selective, yes, always selective, but that does not preclude affection. And it makes
it all the more meaningful when they do choose to spend some precious time with us.

VICKI CROKE
Cats Up Close

My friend, the thought of you will be a new motive for every right action.
What wealth it is to have such friends that we cannot think
of them without elevation!

HENRY DAVID THOREAU

When we love a cat, and touch its life, we exercise that faculty that could,
if so directed, enable us to love others, and to touch their lives as well.

CHARLES BURKE

Stately, kindly, lordly friend,
Condescend
Here to sit by me, and turn
Glorious eyes that smile and burn,
Golden eyes, love's lustrous meed,
On the golden pages I read.

All your wondrous wealth of hair,
Dark and fair,
Silken-shaggy, soft and bright
As the clouds and beams of night,
Pays my reverent hand's caress
Back with friendlier gentleness.

Dogs may fawn on all and some
As they come;
You, a friend of loftier mind,
Answer friends along in kind;
Just your foot upon my hand
Softly bids it understand.

ALGERNON CHARLES SWINBURNE
"TO A CAT"

A true friend is someone who thinks that you are a good egg
even though he knows that you are slightly cracked.

BERNARD MELTZER

Tom Quartz is certainly the cunningest kitten I have ever seen.
He is always playing pranks on Jack and I get very nervous lest Jack should
grow too irritated. The other evening they were both in the library—Jack
sleeping before the fire—Tom Quartz scampering about, an exceedingly
playful little wild creature—which is about what he is. He would race across the
floor, then jump upon the curtain or play with the tassel. Suddenly he spied Jack
and galloped up to him. Jack, looking exceedingly sullen and shamed-faced,
jumped out of the way and got upon the sofa, where Tom Quartz instantly
jumped upon him again. Jack suddenly shifted to the other sofa, where Tom
Quartz again went after him. Then Jack started for the door, while Tom made
a rapid turn under the sofa and around the table, and just as Jack reached
the door, leaped on his hind-quarters. Jack bounded forward and away and the
two went tandem out of the room—Jack not reappearing at all; and after
about five minutes Tom Quartz stalked solemnly back.

THEODORE ROOSEVELT
Theodore Roosevelt's Letters to His Children

19

I'd like to be the sort of friend that you have been to me.
I'd like to be the help that you've been always glad to be;
I'd like to mean as much to you each minute of the day,
As you have meant, old friend of mine, to me along the way.

EDGAR A. GUEST

I hesitate to speak of his capacity for friendship and the affectionateness of his nature, for I know from his own reserve that he would not care to have it much talked about. We understood each other perfectly, but we never made any fuss about it; when I spoke his name and snapped my fingers, he came to me; when I returned home at night, he was pretty sure to be waiting for me near the gate, and would rise and saunter along the walk, as if his being there were purely accidental—so shy was he commonly of showing feeling…His friendship was rather constant than demonstrative…He liked companionship, but he wouldn't be petted, or fussed over, or sit in anyone's lap a moment…If there was any petting to be done, however, he chose to do it. Often he would sit looking at me, and then, moved by a delicate affection, come and pull at my coat and sleeve until he could touch my face with his nose, and then go away contented.

CHARLES DUDLEY WARNER
Calvin, the Cat

21

Friendship is the greatest of worldly goods.
Certainly to me it is the chief happiness of life.

C. S. LEWIS

Whenever he was out of luck and a little downhearted,
he would fall to mourning over the loss of a wonderful cat he used to own
(for where women and children are not, men of kindly impulses take up with
pets, for they must love something). And he always spoke of the strange sagacity
of that cat with the air of a man who believed in his secret heart that there was
something human about it…

MARK TWAIN
Dick Baker's Cat

Friendship…is a union of spirits, a marriage of hearts
and the bond thereto virtue.

WILLIAM PENN

The fat cat, still sitting on the mat, smiled at them, as if to show she didn't mind the joke being on her. Then she saw Corporal Randy Jones, and for some reason known only to herself ran toward him as though he were her long-lost master. With a refrigerator purr, she weaved in and out of his muddy legs.

Everyone laughed again as Randy picked her up and pushed his ugly face against the sleek fur. It was funny to see any living thing show a preference for the dour, solitary Randy.

A sergeant flicked his fingers. "Kitty. Come here. We'll make you B Company mascot."

But the cat, perched on Randy's shoulder like a queen on her throne, merely smiled down majestically as much as to say: "You can be my subjects if you like. But this is my man—my royal consort."

And never for a second did she swerve from her devotion. She lived with Randy, slept with him, ate only food provided by him. Almost every man in Company B tried to seduce her with caresses and morsels of canned ration, but all advances were met with a yawn of contempt.

For Randy, this new love was ecstasy. He guarded her with the possessive tenderness of a mother. He combed her fur sleek; he almost starved himself to maintain her fatness. And all the time there was a strange wonder in him. The homeliest and ungainliest of ten in a West Virginia mining family, he had never before aroused affection in man or woman. No one had counted for him until the fat cat.

Q. PATRICK
The Fat Cat

A reassuring presence,
A light when times are dark,
A hand reaching out,
Is what friendship is about.

AUTHOR UNKNOWN

Those who love cats which do not even purr,
Or which are thin and tired and very old,
Bend down to them in the street and stroke their fur
And rub the ears and smooth their breast, and hold
Their paws, and gaze into their eyes of gold.

FRANCES SCARFE
"CATS"

I shall never forget the indulgence with which Dr. Johnson treated Hodge
his cat, for whom he himself used to go out and buy oysters, lest the servants,
having that trouble, should take a dislike to the poor creature.

JAMES BOSWELL
Life of Dr. Johnson

Rest content with my friendship,
for I say once more that is all I can promise,
and I will promise no more than I can bestow.

ALEXANDRE DUMAS
The Count of Monte Cristo

29

But even for an English cat this cat was exceptionally friendly and fine—especially friendly. It leapt at one graceful bound into my lap, nestled there, put out an engaging right front paw to touch my arm with a pretty timidity by way of introduction, rolled up at me an eye of bright but innocent affection, and then smiled a secret smile of approval.

HILAIRE BELLOC
A Conversation With a Cat

I will always remember the olive-eyed tabby who taught me that not all relationships are meant to last a lifetime. Sometimes just an hour is enough to touch your heart.

BARBARA L. DIAMOND

31

I want a warm and faithful friend,
To cheer the adverse hour;
Who ne'er to flatter will descend,
Not bend the knee to power.
A friend to chide me when I'm wrong,
My inmost soul to see;
And that my friendship prove as strong
To him as his to me.

JOHN QUINCY ADAMS

Animals are such agreeable friends—they ask no questions,
they pass no criticisms.

GEORGE ELIOT

One evening we were all, except father, going to a ball, and when we started, left "the master" and his cat in the drawing-room together. "The master" was reading at a small table, on which a lighted candle was placed. Suddenly the candle went out. My father, who was much interested in his book, relighted the candle, stroked the cat, who was looking at him pathetically he noticed, and continued his reading. A few minutes later, as the light became dim, he looked up just in time to see puss deliberately put out the candle with his paw, and then look appealingly toward him. This second and unmistakable hint was not disregarded, and puss was given the petting he craved. Father was full of this anecdote when all met at breakfast the next morning.

MAMIE DICKENS
My Father As I Recall Him

The most I can do for my friend is simply to be his friend.
I have no wealth to bestow on him. If he knows that I am happy in loving him, he will want no other reward. Is not friendship divine in this?

HENRY DAVID THOREAU

Sometimes people come into your life and you know right away that they are meant to be there; they serve some sort of purpose, teach you a lesson, or help you figure out who you are.

AUTHOR UNKNOWN

In Florence, a rich and famous city of Italy in the province called Tuscany, there lived two gentlemen of wealth and quality, Anselmo and Lothario, such great friends that by way of distinction they were called by all that knew them "The Two Friends." They were unmarried, young, of the same age and of the same tastes, which was enough to account for the reciprocal friendship between them.

MIGUEL CERVANTES
Don Quixote

Royalty resides in my home. A furry four-footed feline is sovereign over all that she can see from the back of her sofa-sized throne. For all her obvious superiority, she has been long suffering enough to allow me to be her favored lady-in-waiting.

MICHELLE PLAUNTY

No friendship is an accident.

O HENRY

In friendship…we think we have chosen our peers. In reality, a few years difference in the date of our births, a few more miles between certain houses, the choice of one university instead of another, posting to different regiments, the accident of a topic being raised or not raised at a first meeting—any of these chances might have kept us apart. But…there are, strictly speaking, no chances. A secret Master of Ceremonies has been at work…The Friendship is not a reward for our discrimination and good taste in finding one another out. It is the instrument by which God reveals to each the beauties of all others. They are no greater than the beauties of a thousand other men; by Friendship God opens our eyes to them. They are, like all beauties, derived from Him, and then, in a good Friendship, increased by time through the Friendship itself, so that it is His instrument for creation as well as for revealing.

C.S. LEWIS
The Four Loves

Friendships are the best books in the library of life.

WALLACE RICE

Dear friends, let us love one another, for love comes from God.
Everyone who loves has been born of God and knows God.

THE BOOK OF 1 JOHN

We are not strangers, we are neighbors, and you [Laurie] needn't think
you'd be a bother. We want to know you, and I've been trying to do it
this ever so long. We haven't been here a great while, you know,
but we have got acquainted with all our neighbors but you.

LOUISA MAY ALCOTT
Little Women

There was a sound between them. A warm and contented sound
like the murmur of giant bees in a hollow tree.

STEPHEN VINCENT BENET

Think where man's glory most begins and ends,
And say my glory was I had such friends.

WILLIAM BUTLER YEATS

As the two boys walked sorrowing along, they made a new compact
to stand by each other and be brothers and never separate
till death relieved them of their troubles.

MARK TWAIN
The Adventures of Tom Sawyer

Time passed on, and one morning Gon lay before the house door,
basking in the sun. He looked lazily at the world stretched out before him,
and saw in the distance a big ruffian of a cat tearing and ill-treating quite a little
one. He jumped up, fully of rage, and chased away the big cat, and then he turned
to comfort the little one, when his heart nearly burst with joy to find that it was
Koma. At first Koma did not know him again, he had grown so large and stately;
but when it dawned upon her who it was, her happiness knew no bounds.
And they rubbed their heads and their noses again and again, while their
purring might have been heard a mile off.

DAVID BRAUN
The Cat's Elopement

I said a prayer for you today,
And I know God must have heard,
I felt the answer in my heart
Although He spoke no word…
I asked that He'd be near you
At the start of each new day,
To grant you health and blessings
And friends to share your way.
I asked for happiness for you
In all things great and small,
But it was for His loving care
I prayed the most of all.

MARGARET GOULD

When all of life seems unsteady
And it's hard to grasp the now,
I find calm assurance in our friendship;
You are, to me, the cat's meow.

VERONICA CURTIS